THURGOOD MARSHALL

SUPREME COURT JUSTICE

"The battle has not yet been won;
we have barely begun....
America has no choice but to do better
to assure justice for all Americans,
Afro and white, rich and poor,
educated and illiterate....
Our futures are bound together."
— Thurgood Marshall —

BY CARLA WILLIAMS

Published by The Child's World®
1980 Lookout Drive • Mankato, MN 56003-1705
800-599-READ • www.childsworld.com

PHOTOS

Cover and page 4: AP Photo
Interior: AP Photo: 20, 24; Bettmann via Getty Images: 23; Detroit Publishing Co./Library of Congress, Prints and Photographs Division: 7; Everett Collection/ Newscom: 10, 13, 14, 17, 18, 28 (both); Everett Collection/Shutterstock.com: 8; KEYSTONE Pictures USA/ZUMA Press/Newscom: 6; LBJ Library photo by Yoichi Okamoto: 5, 21, 29; Library of Congress, Prints and Photographs Division: 12; Marion S. Trikosko/Library of Congress, Prints and Photographs Division: 22; Montgomery County Sheriff's Dept./ZUMA Press/Newscom: 19; Robert S. Oakes/Library of Congress, Prints and Photographs Division: 27, 31; Robert Trippett/ZUMA Press/ Newscom: 25; Russell Lee/Library of Congress, Prints and Photographs Division: 11; Schomburg Center for Research in Black Culture, Photographs and Prints Division, The New York Public Library: 9; W. Scott McGill/Shutterstock.com: 26

LIBRARY OF CONGRESS CATALOGING-IN-PUBLICATION DATA

ISBN 9781503854505 (Reinforced Library Binding)
ISBN 9781503854970 (Portable Document Format)
ISBN 9781503855359 (Online Multi-user eBook)
LCCN: 2021930417

Printed in the United States of America

Cover and page 4 caption:
Thurgood Marshall in 1962.

CONTENTS

Chapter One

FROM TROUBLEMAKER TO HONOR STUDENT

Thoroughgood Marshall was born in Baltimore, Maryland, on July 2, 1908. His father, William, was a waiter and a steward. As a steward, William was in charge of the other Black workers at his job. At the time, it was a good job for a Black man to have. Thoroughgood's mother, Norma, was a schoolteacher. Thoroughgood had one older brother named William Jr., who was called by his middle name, Aubrey.

Norma and William Marshall knew that education was very important for their sons. Norma made sure they went to school. She wanted them to succeed and never let them give up. William had not been able to finish school when he was young. He always regretted this because he had wanted to be a lawyer. He liked to **debate** and argue with his sons at dinner. In this way, he taught them to think about what they said.

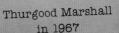

Thurgood Marshall in 1967

William wanted his sons to be able to speak intelligently about anything. It was an early lesson for Thoroughgood that would be important later in his life. The dinnertime debates with his father made Thoroughgood want to become a lawyer.

Thoroughgood Marshall at age 2.

Thoroughgood was named after his grandfather, Thoroughgood 'Thorney" Marshall. Thorney was born enslaved. The Marshall family liked to tell the story that Thorney was so disobedient, his enslaver had to set him free. In truth, Thorney escaped slavery when he was about 14 years old. He then went to live in Baltimore. Many of the Black people who lived there were not enslaved. They had escaped, been set free, or otherwise attained their freedom.

Thorney worked as a waiter after he escaped. Soon he joined the U.S. Army and went to Texas. When he returned to Baltimore, he opened a grocery store. Thoroughgood was just as independent as Thorney. As a child, he tired of spelling his long name and began to spell it 'Thurgood." He even got his mother to change the spelling on his birth certificate. Thurgood's nickname was "Goody."

Thurgood's other grandfather, Isaiah Williams, was born free. Unlike most African Americans at that time, he was never enslaved. Isaiah joined the U.S. Navy and worked for a ship's captain during the U.S. Civil War (1861–1865). After the war, Isaiah became a businessperson. He owned two grocery stores in Baltimore. Isaiah Williams believed that all people in the United States should have **civil rights**. He knew that all people were equal, no matter what color their skin was. He often said that Black children should be allowed to go to public schools. He did not know that one day his grandson would be the person to make this possible.

Both of Thurgood's grandmothers, Annie Robinson and Mary Fossett, were born free in Baltimore. Both women could read and write. Many Black people were not given the chance to learn these skills. In fact, for enslaved people, learning to read and write was against the law. Thurgood's parents and grandparents believed in equality for everyone. They taught this belief to Thurgood and his brother Aubrey.

The Marshall boys grew up with both Black and white neighbors. This was unusual at the time. Most places in the United States were **segregated**—Black people lived separately from white people.

Baltimore, Maryland in 1906

As a young boy, Thurgood was the class troublemaker. He did not work at his studies but preferred to read detective stories. Thurgood's school was next door to the police station. He could look out of his classroom window and see the prisoners. He noticed that Black people were not treated fairly. In fact, the police often beat them. Thurgood knew this was wrong. He began to think more about becoming a lawyer. He thought that laws should be changed to protect Black people.

Thurgood began to work harder in school. He got better grades, but he did not stop playing around. In high school, he was still getting into trouble. To punish him, his teachers made him read the **Constitution** of the United States. Thurgood was in trouble a lot. By the time he graduated from high school, he had learned the whole Constitution by heart!

Students at an all-Black high school in Oklahoma in 1917.

Thurgood went to college at Lincoln University in Pennsylvania— the first American university for Black students. His brother Aubrey was also a student at Lincoln. Aubrey was studying to become a doctor. The two Marshall boys were quite different. Aubrey was a quiet boy, but Thurgood spoke loudly. Thurgood played cards and read comic books. He watched cowboy movies. He was a popular and fun student at Lincoln.

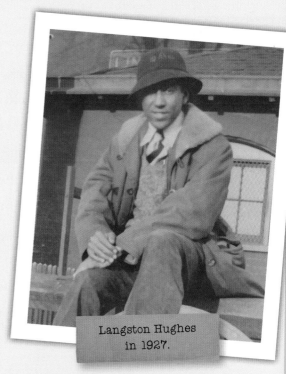

Langston Hughes
in 1927.

The Marshalls had protected Aubrey and Thurgood from **racism**. The brothers did not fully realize how unfairly Black people were treated. Thurgood did not know just how much some Americans disliked Black people. They disliked them so much, they did not want to be near them. A man named Langston Hughes was Thurgood's classmate at Lincoln. Langston was already a famous poet when he went to college. The other students looked up to him. He taught Thurgood a very important lesson.

The students at Lincoln voted on whether to have both white and Black teachers. Thurgood and most of the other students voted that they did not want Black teachers. Sadly, they believed that whites would be better teachers. But Langston Hughes voted in favor of Black teachers. He thought that Black students should have Black role models.

Langston Hughes was born James Mercer Langston Hughes in 1902. He moved from Joplin, Missouri, to New York City as a young man. He soon became well known for his writing as well as his activism. Hughes was a major influence on Marshall on topics of race and equality.

Langston knew that having teachers who looked like them would make the students feel proud. He also knew that Black teachers should have the same chance to teach as white teachers. Langston wrote a school paper to say so. He gave talks to the other students. Thurgood began to agree with Langston. He realized that change could happen if people worked together. The next time there was a vote, Thurgood voted for the Black teachers. A Black teacher started to work at the school the following year. Thurgood also became more serious about his studies.

In his senior year, Thurgood met 17-year-old Vivian Burey. Her nickname was "Buster." Buster was from Philadelphia. She was a student at the University of Pennsylvania. The couple married in her hometown. They rented a small apartment in Oxford, near Lincoln University. Twenty-year-old Thurgood went back to Lincoln to finish college. He spent even more time studying. The next year, he graduated from college with honors. He began to think about going to law school.

Thurgood at about 30 years old.

Chapter Two

LAWYER AND CIVIL RIGHTS CHAMP

After graduating from college, Thurgood Marshall moved back to Baltimore. He and his wife lived with his parents. Marshall wanted to go to the University of Maryland Law School, but it did not accept African American students. That made him angry. He knew it was not fair to keep him out just because he was Black.

Jim Crow laws forced Black peo drink from separate water coo

At this time, white people and Black people still experienced segregation in many states. They could not live next door to one another. They could not go to school together. In some states, they could not even drink from the same water fountains. The laws and customs that enforced this separation were called "Jim Crow." (Jim Crow was a Black character in a **minstrel** show, but no one is sure how the term came to mean segregation.) Many people—including Thurgood Marshall—knew the Jim Crow laws were wrong. They wanted to do away with them for good.

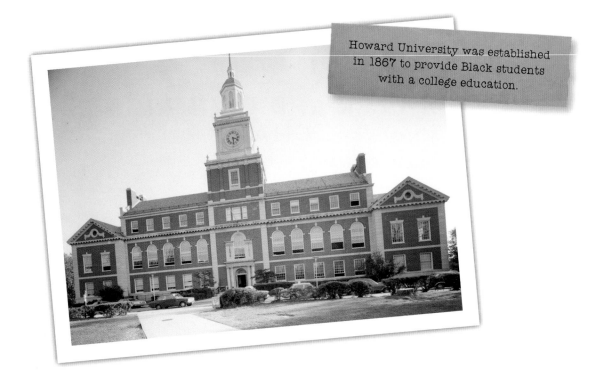

Howard University was established in 1867 to provide Black students with a college education.

Marshall went to Howard University Law School in Washington, DC. He took a job in the school's law library. That way, he could study the law even when he was at work. The **Supreme Court** of the United States is also located in Washington, DC. While he was a law student, Marshall sometimes skipped class. He went to the Supreme Court to listen to the lawyers present their **cases**. He heard some of the best lawyers in the country argue their cases before the Supreme Court. Marshall wanted to become one of those lawyers.

In law school, Marshall met Charles Hamilton Houston. Houston was the new **dean** of the law school. He was a stiff and proper man. Some of the students were afraid of him. He was a tough teacher who wanted only the best work from his students.

Houston had been the first African American lawyer to argue a case before the Supreme Court. He taught his students that they would gain civil rights only by changing laws. He believed that segregation went against the U.S. Constitution. He believed in **integration**—in white and Black people living and going to school together. Mr. Houston became Marshall's role model. Marshall worked hard in law school. He graduated first in his class, with the best grades of all the students.

Howard University has had many noted graduates. Elijah Cummings, Toni Morrison, Paul Laurence Dunbar, Zora Neale Hurston, Chadwick Boseman, Taraji P. Henson, and Vice President Kamala Harris all graduated from Howard.

In 1933, Marshall earned his law degree and opened his own law office in Baltimore. At that time, people were very poor. It was a period known as the **Great Depression**, when there was little business activity. Many of the people who came to Marshall for help could not pay him. He took their cases anyway. He kept working hard. He soon began to get clients who could pay.

In 1934, Marshall went to work for the National Association for the Advancement of Colored People (NAACP). The NAACP wanted civil rights for all Americans. To achieve this, it needed good lawyers to win cases in court. Thurgood and Buster Marshall moved to New York City for his new job.

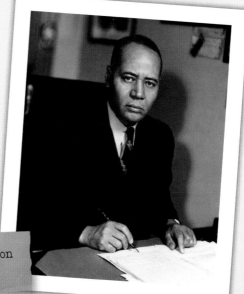

Charles Hamilton Houston at his desk in 1939.

It still bothered Marshall that he had not been allowed to attend the University of Maryland Law School. He wanted to take the school to court. He believed the law would prove that segregation was wrong.

In 1936, an African American man **sued** the University of Maryland for refusing to admit him. Marshall and Charles Houston took his case. They argued against segregation and won. The University of Maryland finally agreed to admit African American students. It was a personal and public victory for Marshall. Even though it was too late for him to go to school there, he had made sure that no other Black students would be turned away because of their skin color. Marshall's next big case was to make sure that Black teachers in Maryland earned the same pay as white teachers. His mother was a teacher. He knew she worked as hard as the white teachers. He won that case, too.

By 1940, Marshall was head of the NAACP Legal Defense and Educational Fund. But he did not get to stay at home in New York. To raise money for the Fund and to work on cases, he traveled 50,000 miles per year. In his early years with the NAACP, Marshall tried many cases. A number of these were filed to integrate schools. Some of Marshall's cases were for serious crimes, such as murder. Often his clients were innocent.

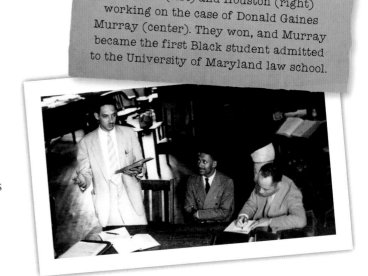

Marshall (left) and Houston (right) working on the case of Donald Gaines Murray (center). They won, and Murray became the first Black student admitted to the University of Maryland law school.

Marshall did not win every case, however. Sometimes innocent people were put to death. Marshall did not believe in the **death penalty**. He believed that death was not a fair punishment for any crime. He knew that Black and poor people were given the death penalty more often than anyone else. The death penalty was often a result of racism and **prejudice**. Losing these cases made him work even harder to win.

Marshall believed that all public places in the United States should be integrated. He knew that the best way to make this happen was to focus on one thing first. He decided to concentrate on integrating schools.

Marshall became the head lawyer in a 1954 lawsuit known as *Brown versus the Board of Education of Topeka* (Kansas). Reverend Oliver Brown was an African American father in Topeka who sued the school board. His daughter, Linda, had to cross the railroad tracks to get to school. This was too dangerous for a little girl. Reverend Brown wanted Linda to be able to go to the public school closest to their home.

Leaders of the Topeka NAACP asked other African American parents to be part of a case as well. Soon, 13 families agreed to take part in the challenge to end segregation in public schools. The case was brought before the Supreme Court. All nine judges on the Court **ruled** in favor of ending school segregation. They stated, "Does segregation of children in public schools solely on the basis of race ... deprive the children of the **minority** group of equal educational opportunities? We believe that it does."

The NAACP was founded in 1909 to help enforce legal rights guaranteed by the Constitution and to put an end to violence against Black people, especially the brutal practice of lynching. Today, the NAACP is the oldest and largest civil rights organization in the nation. It continues its mission to ensure equal rights for all and fight back against discrimination based on race.

Here are the words to the song "Thurgood Marshall, Mr. Civil Rights" (sung to the tune of "The Ballad of Davy Crockett")

Thurgood...
Thurgood Marshall,
Mr. Civil Rights.
Born in Maryland,
The state of the free,
Went to Howard for his law degree,
Took his training at Charlie's knee,
Said, "It isn't so free, as you can see."
Thurgood...
Thurgood Marshall,
Mr. Civil Rights.
Fought for the teachers,
Fought for the schools,
Went down South
Where they broke all the rules,
Now he's working on the swimming pools,
Justice and right are his fighting tools.
Thurgood...
Thurgood Marshall,
Mr. Civil Rights.

The country was shocked. Such a ruling had never been made before. African Americans were very happy. Marshall became a hero. *Brown versus the Board of Education of Topeka* was one of the most important court cases in U.S. history. Marshall was so famous that a song was made up about him.

While Marshall was busy at work on court cases, his wife Buster became sick. She did not want to worry her husband, so she did not tell him how sick she really was. Not long after Marshall won the famous case, Buster told him she had cancer.

Throughout their marriage, Marshall's job had required him to travel most of the time. Sometimes he was gone for weeks. His wife's cancer shocked him. He regretted having spent so much time away from home in the previous years. He had known she was sick but had not known how serious it was. He loved his wife very much. He decided to stay at home to care for her in the last months of her life. Buster Marshall died on her birthday in 1955. She was 44 years old. The couple had been married for 25 years, and her death left Marshall very sad.

Chapter Three

THE SUPREME COURT

Some time after Buster Marshall's death, Marshall began to see a young woman named Cecilia Suyat. She was a secretary at the NAACP. Everyone called her Cissy. She was born in Hawaii, and her parents were from the Philippines. Cissy and Thurgood fell in love and were married. They had two sons. Marshall was pleased, for he had always wanted to have at least one son. The elder boy, Thurgood Jr., was nicknamed "Goody" after his father. The younger son was named John William. For many years, Marshall had worked hard for civil rights. Now he spent time with his new family. He loved to play with his sons and his model trains. For the first time, Marshall took a break from work to enjoy his life.

Marshall was not the only person working for equality in the United States. All across the country, the **Civil Rights Movement** was growing. New leaders, such as the Reverend Martin Luther King Jr., were starting to be noticed.

Marshall a
Cissy with
two sons in

King was a preacher who worked in Montgomery, Alabama. In December of 1955, an African American woman in Montgomery named Rosa Parks was told to give up her bus seat to a white person. A law required Black passengers to sit in the back of buses. It also required them to give up their seats to whites if there were not enough seats for everybody. But Rosa Parks and other Black citizens were tired of such inequality. She said "No," and was arrested.

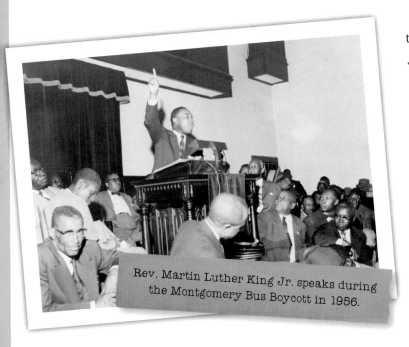

Rev. Martin Luther King Jr. speaks during the Montgomery Bus Boycott in 1956.

Black people knew that Rosa Parks's arrest was wrong. If Black riders paid the same fare as everyone else, they shouldn't be forced to ride at the back of the bus or to stand. Reverend King urged Black people to start a **protest**—a **boycott** of the public buses.

The Montgomery boycott lasted for 382 days. The city did not back down, even though it lost a lot of money from the bus fares. Thurgood Marshall did not believe in protests. He knew they could be dangerous for Black people. Instead, he believed in fighting prejudice through the court system.

Marshall and the NAACP supported Rosa Parks's case and even took it to the Supreme Court. Once again, the NAACP won a case to end segregation. Afterward, Reverend King became the first Black man to ride on one of Montgomery's newly integrated buses. He also became famous as a civil rights leader.

Marshall decided that he needed a break from his job. Black leaders in the African country of Kenya invited him to visit their nation. They asked him to help them write a new constitution.

Rosa Parks's booking photo, taken on February 22, 1956.

Marshall thought that the U.S. Constitution was the best in the world. He felt that it should apply to everyone, no matter what their color or race. Marshall based Kenya's constitution on the U.S. Constitution. He was proud to help the Kenyan people.

When he returned from Kenya, Marshall learned that students in the South had begun to hold **sit-ins** at lunch counters. They wanted to desegregate them. The students would go into a restaurant and sit at the counter. They would ask nicely to be served. When they were told no and asked to leave, they refused to move. Then the police arrested them. The students wanted to be arrested.

The protesters believed they could change the law only by being arrested and going to court. Only by going to court could the law be changed. More than 1,700 students were arrested at sit-ins during the Civil Rights Movement. Marshall still did not approve of protests. He was afraid that they were unsafe and could become violent. But he agreed to defend the students before the Supreme Court. The Court ruled in favor of Marshall and the students, ending segregation in restaurants.

By this time, Marshall was 53 years old. He was known around the world as "Mr. Civil Rights." He was the most famous and important lawyer in the

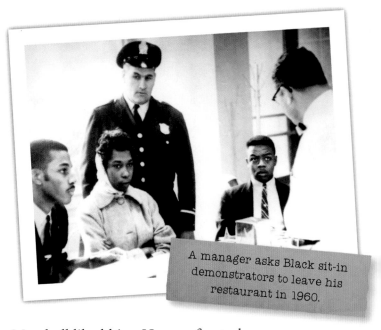

A manager asks Black sit-in demonstrators to leave his restaurant in 1960.

country. Most people who met Marshall liked him. He was fun to be around and had lots of charm. He could talk to anybody and liked to tell good stories. Even some people who were prejudiced against African Americans liked him. Marshall's easy manner helped him win cases. He had worked for the NAACP for 25 years. In that time he had won 29 of the 32 cases he had argued before the U.S. Supreme Court. Judges and other lawyers liked him. Marshall knew when to talk about the law, and he knew when to talk like an ordinary person.

President John F. Kennedy knew that Thurgood Marshall was
a good lawyer. In 1961, he offered Marshall a new job as a **federal**
judge on the U.S. Second Circuit Court of **Appeals** in New York City.
Marshall became the first African American ever to serve on this court.
This was an important job. Sometimes when people go to court, they
do not believe the judge has ruled fairly. They can appeal their case and
have the ruling reviewed by a higher court. As an appeals court judge,
Marshall wrote 112 court decisions.

The Supreme Court, the highest
court in the land, has never overturned or
reversed any of those decisions. Marshall
served as a federal judge for several years.
Then one day, he received a phone call.
President Lyndon Baines Johnson wanted
him to be the U.S. **Solicitor** General. The
job of the Solicitor General is to argue
the national government's side in cases
before the Supreme Court. No African
American had ever held such a high-
level government job. Marshall was
excited about his new job but also a little worried.
His job as a judge was for life. He could not be fired or replaced. But
if he took the job as Solicitor General, the next president could replace
him. He would also earn less money. But it was not every day that the
president of the United States called to offer a job. Marshall accepted.

Marshall and President
Lyndon Baines
Johnson in 1965.

Thurgood Marshall was an effective Solicitor General. He won 14 out of the 19 cases he argued before the Supreme Court. In fact, Marshall argued and won more cases before the Supreme Court than anyone else. As Solicitor General, he continued to fight **discrimination**.

President Johnson was pleased with Marshall. The two men got along well and became friends. They were both big, tall men. They were easygoing and liked to share jokes and tell wild stories. But their lives were not all fun and jokes. Both men worked hard for civil rights. Each respected the other. Johnson decided to offer Marshall an even more important position.

In 1967, President Johnson **appointed** Marshall to the Supreme Court as a **justice**. Nine judges sit on the Supreme Court. Marshall's first words upon hearing the news were "Oh, yipe!" He was very surprised. It was his lifelong dream

Marshall being sworn in as Solicitor General in 1965.

come true. In law school, he used to go to the Supreme Court to hear the cases. From that time on, Marshall had wanted to be a Supreme Court justice. Now it had actually happened.

As a justice, Marshall kept working for civil rights for all Americans. He included poor and homeless people in his fight for civil rights. He also worked for the rights of prisoners. He believed strongly in affirmative action. This meant that the government would "affirm" or say

Thurgood (back row, right) with the other Supreme Court justices in 1967.

"yes" to giving people in minority groups an equal chance for jobs and education. Marshall knew that all people were not fair in their hearts. Affirmative action made sure that they treated others fairly by law. Minority people were not just Black people. They were all people who belonged to a smaller group within the population. Asian and Latino people were minorities. Even women were considered minorities because they often did not have the same opportunities as men. All minorities gained from affirmative action. It gave more Americans an equal start in life.

When Marshall first became a Supreme Court justice, most of the other justices agreed with him on important court decisions. He was a Supreme Court justice for 24 years. During this time, all of the other justices retired or passed away. New presidents appointed new justices. In time, Marshall found that he was in the minority on the Court. Some of the new justices did not believe in affirmative action. Their ideas about civil rights were different from his. The country began to change.

Chapter Four

THURGOOD MARSHALL'S LEGACY

As Marshall grew older, people recognized his hard work for civil rights. They began to build monuments in his honor and name schools after him. The University of Maryland renamed their law school after Thurgood Marshall. This did not please him. Fifty years earlier, this same school had refused to admit him because he was Black. He was still angry that he hadn't been allowed to go there. But to most other people, the renamed law school was a sign of progress. It made many Americans proud to have a school named after a Black person.

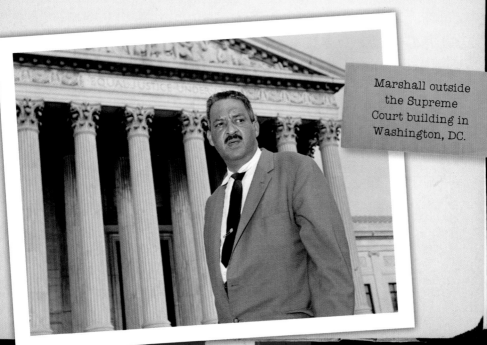

Marshall outside the Supreme Court building in Washington, DC.

Marshall posed for a sculptor to make a statue of him. It stands in front of the federal building in his hometown of Baltimore. He also gave all of his notes and papers from his entire career to the Library of

Marshall (front row, second from right) and the other Supreme Court justices in 1990.

Congress. By doing so, he made sure that students could study all of his legal ideas and decisions for years to come.

Marshall served as a Supreme Court justice from October 2, 1967, until October 1, 1991. During that time, he saw many changes in the country and on the Court. Six different presidents held office while Marshall sat on the bench. Marshall had once said that he would serve out his life term as a justice.

But times had changed. For a long time, he had been in poor health. He finally **resigned** from the Supreme Court in 1991. President George Bush appointed Clarence Thomas to replace Marshall. Thomas was also an African American, but he did not agree with Marshall's views on equality and civil rights. Thomas did not believe in affirmative action. In fact, he did not think that the *Brown versus the Board of Education of Topeka* decision was correct. Being replaced by Thomas made Marshall unhappy. He did not want all of his hard work to come undone after he retired.

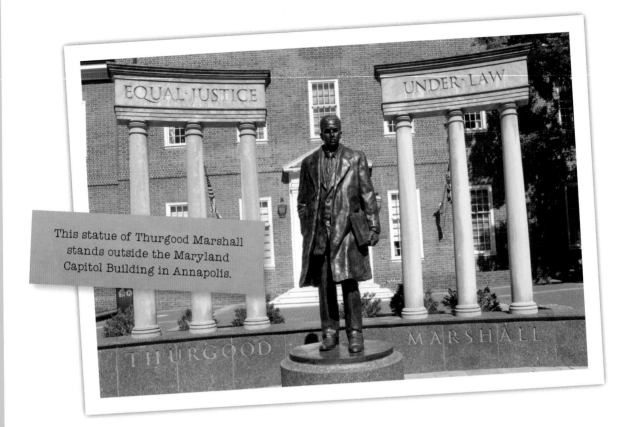

This statue of Thurgood Marshall stands outside the Maryland Capitol Building in Annapolis.

Thurgood Marshall died on January 24, 1993. He was 84 years old. Thousands of people from all over the country went to Washington, DC, to pay their respects. Many people believe that through his legal work, Marshall did more for equality in the United States than anyone else. He also set a strong example for his sons to follow. His son Thurgood Jr. is a lawyer. Marshall's son John William became a police officer.

At Monroe Elementary School in Topeka, Kansas, is the *Brown versus the Board of Education of Topeka* National Historic Site. It honors the 1954 Supreme Court decision that desegregated the public schools. Monroe is the school that Oliver Brown had wanted his daughter Linda to attend.

Thurgood Marshall never called himself an African American. He did not call himself Black. He came from an earlier time when people used the words "Negro" and "colored." He used those terms all his life. When he was older, he sometimes used the term "Afro-American." It did not matter what words Marshall used to describe himself. He knew that all men and women are equal. Words could not limit that equality, and he never let words limit him. Look around your neighborhood or school. Are there students there of a different color or race than you? If so, then Thurgood Marshall is one of the reasons why you and your friends of different colors and races can live and learn together.

After Thurgood Marshall died, a former assistant wrote that he "had the capacity to imagine a radically different world... and the courage and ability to make that imagined world real."

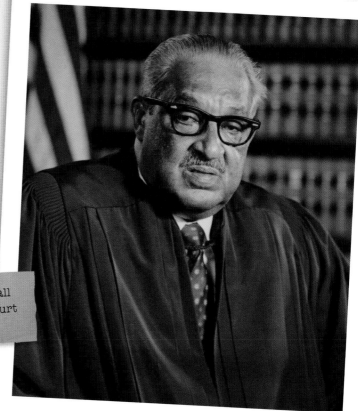

Thurgood Marshall in his Supreme Court robe in 1976

27

What would happen if your school was just for white students or just for Black and other students of color?
Would some of your friends, teachers, or school
leaders change, or would they stay the same?
How does being in a school with kids from different
races and ethnicities change your experience?

What are the arguments for affirmative action?
What are arguments against it?
Do you think affirmative action laws are important to have?

TIME LINE

1900-1920

1908
Thoroughgood Marshall is born in Baltimore, Maryland, on July 2. As a little boy, he changes the spelling of his name to "Thurgood."

1926
Marshall goes to college at Lincoln University in Pennsylvania. He becomes friends with the famous poet Langston Hughes, who teaches him about prejudice.

1929
Marshall marries Vivian "Buster" Burey.

1930

1930
Marshall graduates from Lincoln University with honors. He enrolls at Howard University and meets Charles Hamilton Houston, who will become his role model.

1933
Marshall receives his law degree from Howard University.

1934
Marshall goes to work for the NAACP. As an NAACP lawyer, he will win many important cases in the next 25 years.

1936
Marshall argues and wins the case that desegregates the University of Maryland.

1940

1940
The NAACP names Marshall the head of its Legal Defense and Educational Fund.

**Marshall did not believe in the death penalty because
it was often a result of racism and prejudice.**
Do you think a person should be put to death if they killed someone?
Does it matter how the person who died was killed?
What if the penalty for a crime changes depending on the
color of a person's skin, or how much money the person has?

How would you put Marshall's accomplishments into your own words?
Explain the reasons for your answer.

1950

1954
The Supreme Court rules on the case of *Brown versus the Board of Education of Topeka* to end segregation in all public schools.

1955
Marshall marries Cecilia "Cissy" Suyat. In December, Rosa Parks is arrested in Montgomery, Alabama, for refusing to give up her bus seat to a white person.

1956
Black people in Montgomery boycott the city's buses to protest segregation. The NAACP argues the case that desegregates Montgomery's buses.

1960

1960
Marshall travels to Kenya to help its government write a constitution. He bases it on the U.S. Constitution.

1961
President Kennedy appoints Marshall to be a federal judge in the Second District Court of Appeals in New York City.

1965
Marshall becomes the first African American to be appointed U.S. Solicitor General.

1967
Marshall becomes the first African American appointed to the U.S. Supreme Court. He continues his work to guarantee civil rights to all Americans.

1990

1991
In poor health, Thurgood Marshall retires from the Supreme Court.

1992
President George H. W. Bush names Monroe Elementary School in Topeka, Kansas, a National Historic Site.

1993
Thurgood Marshall dies at age 84. Thousands of people mourn his death and the passing of an important civil rights leader.

appeal (uh-PEEL)
In law, to appeal is to ask a higher court to review a judge's ruling on a case. Thurgood Marshall's first appointment as a judge was in a court of appeals.

appointed (uh-POYNT-ed)
When someone is appointed to a position, he or she is officially chosen and asked to accept. President Johnson appointed Marshall to be a Supreme Court justice.

boycott (BOY-kot)
A boycott is a protest in which people stop using a certain product or service. A boycott helped end segregation on public buses in the city of Montgomery, Alabama.

cases (KAY-sez)
Cases are matters for a court of law to decide. As a law student, Thurgood Marshall would go to the Supreme Court and listen to lawyers present their cases.

civil rights (SIV-el RYTS)
Civil rights are a person's rights to freedom and equal treatment. Marshall believed that Americans of all races should be guaranteed civil rights.

**Civil Rights Movement
(SIV-il RYTZ MOOV-ment)**
The Civil Rights Movement was the struggle for equal rights for African Americans in the United States during the 1950s and 1960s. Martin Luther King Jr. was a leader in the Civil Rights Movement.

Constitution (kon-stih-TOO-shun)
A constitution is a document that lays out how a nation's government and laws will work. Thurgood Marshall read and studied the U.S. Constitution in high school.

dean (DEEN)
A dean is the head of a college or school at a university. Charles Hamilton Houston was dean of the law school when Marshall attended Howard University.

death penalty (DETH PEN-ul-tee)
When people receive the death penalty, they are sentenced to die as punishment for their crimes. Marshall believed that the death penalty was wrong.

debate (deh-BAYT)
A debate is a discussion between people with different opinions on a subject. William Marshall liked to debate with his sons at dinner.

discrimination (diss-KRIM-uh-NAY-shun)
Discrimination is the act of treating people unfairly based on their race, sex, or background. African Americans faced legal discrimination for many years in the United States.

federal (FED-er-ul)
Federal means having to do with the nation's central government, rather than a state or city government. President Kennedy appointed Marshall to be a federal judge.

**Great Depression
(GRAYT dee- PRESH-un)**
The Great Depression was a period during the 1930s in which there was little business activity in the United States, and many people could not find work. Thurgood Marshall opened his law office during the Great Depression and often helped people for free.

integration (in-teh-GRAY-shun)
Integration means bringing together people who had been kept separate, especially because of race. The court decision called *Brown versus the Board of Education of Topeka* led to the integration of public schools.

justice (JUSS-tiss)
A justice is a judge. Thurgood Marshall was one of the nine justices on the U.S. Supreme Court.

minority (mih-NOR-ih-tee)
A minority is a smaller or less powerful group within a larger society, often of a different race or religion. The U.S. Supreme Court decided that children from minority groups should have equal access to education.

minstrel (MIN -strel)
A minstrel is a performer who sings and dances to entertain people. Jim Crow was a Black character in a minstrel show.

prejudice (PREH-juh-diss)
Prejudice is a negative feeling or opinion about someone without a good reason. Marshall believed in using the court system to fight prejudice and unequal treatment.

protest (PROH-test)
A protest is a public statement or gathering in which people speak out to say something is wrong. During the Civil Rights Movement, Americans attended protests to speak out against the poor treatment of minorities.

racism (RAY-sih-zim)
Racism is a negative feeling or opinion about people because of their race. Norma and William Marshall tried to protect their sons from racism.

resigned (reh-ZYND)
When a person has resigned, he or she has left a job or position by choice. In 1991, Thurgood Marshall resigned after serving on the Supreme Court for 24 years.

rule (ROOL)
When a court rules on a case, it makes a decision. In 1954, all nine judges on the Supreme Court ruled to end segregation in public schools.

segregated (SEG-reh-gay-ted)
If people or things are segregated, they are kept apart. Many places in the United States were once segregated, so that African Americans could not enter areas or were kept separate from white people.

sit-ins (SIT-inz)
A sit-in is a kind of protest in which people sit down and refuse to leave. During the Civil Rights Movement, sit-ins helped end segregation in restaurants.

solicitor (suh-LISS-ih-tur)
A solicitor is a lawyer in a city, state, or national government. As U.S. Solicitor General, Marshall argued the national government's side in cases before the Supreme Court.

sue (SOO)
When people sue other people, they take them to court to resolve a disagreement. When an African American man sued the University of Maryland in 1936, Thurgood Marshall was one of his lawyers.

Supreme Court (suh-PREEM KORT)
The Supreme Court is the highest court in the United States. Thurgood Marshall was a member of the Supreme Court.

BOOKS

Benoit, Peter. *Brown v. Board of Education*. New York, NY: Children's Press, 2013.

Jeffrey, Gary. *Thurgood Marshall: The Supreme Court Rules on "Separate But Equal"*. New York, NY: Gareth Stevens, 2013.

Magoon, Kekla. *The Highest Tribute: Thurgood Marshall's Life, Leadership, and Legacy*. New York, NY: Quill Tree Books, 2021.

Somervill, Barbara A. *Brown v. Board of Education*. Mankato, MN: The Child's World, 2022.

Winter, Jonah. *Thurgood*. New York, NY: Schwartz & Wade Books, 2019.

WEBSITES

Visit our website for links about Thurgood Marshall:

childsworld.com/links

Note to Parents, Teachers, and Librarians: We routinely verify our Web links to make sure they are safe, active sites—so encourage your readers to check them out!